Happy Birthday
Kasey

Grandma & Poppa

Richard Scarry's
BUSY WORKERS

A GOLDEN BOOK • NEW YORK
Western Publishing Company, Inc., Racine, Wisconsin 53404

There are all kinds of busy workers on the street. Some make deliveries and others collect things. Do you see what is being picked up and what is being delivered in front of Mr. Pig's house?

fuel deliveryman

garbage collectors

mail carrier

homeowner

postal worker

MAIL

All around the neighborhood
other busy workers are doing
their jobs.

The police officer is giving
that naughty Dingo a ticket
for speeding.

police officer

sanitation worker

The sanitation worker
is cleaning the street
with his road sweeper.

electricians

vers

Down the street a house has been sold. Eddie and Son,
the electricians, are making repairs before the new owners
arrive. They have to work fast. Do you see why?

Look who just drove up in a big moving van. It's the movers.

Smokey is trying to take
a nap in the firehouse.
Suddenly the fire alarm bell rings.
BBBRRRIIINNNGGG!

fire fighter

Hurry, Smokey. Squeaky Mouse's
house is on fire!

Clang, clang. Watch out! The fire truck is coming through. Officer Murphy stops the traffic.

bus driver

taxi driver

street sweeper

SWOO-O-O-O-SH! Smokey sprays a stream of water at the fire. Squeaky's house is saved!

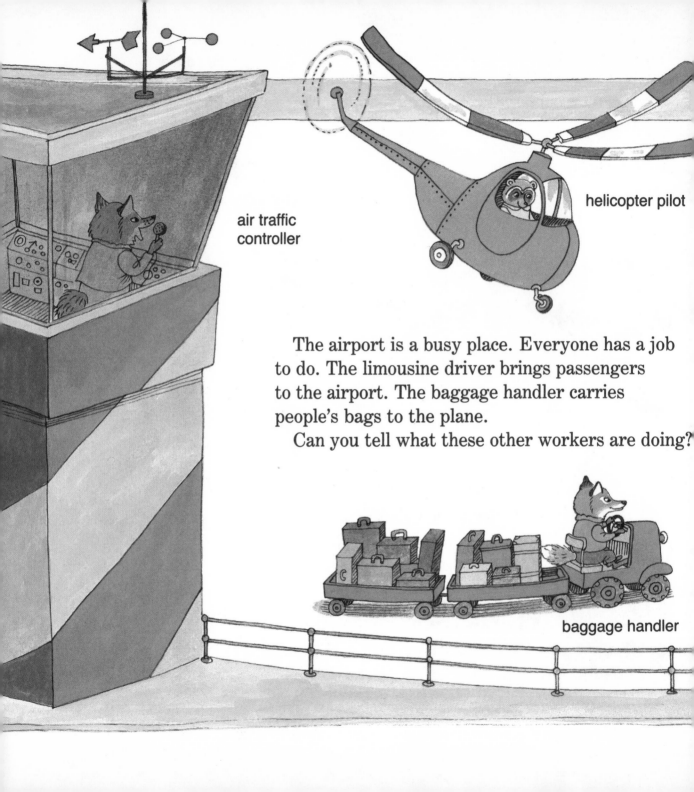

air traffic
controller

helicopter pilot

The airport is a busy place. Everyone has a job
to do. The limousine driver brings passengers
to the airport. The baggage handler carries
people's bags to the plane.

Can you tell what these other workers are doing?

baggage handler

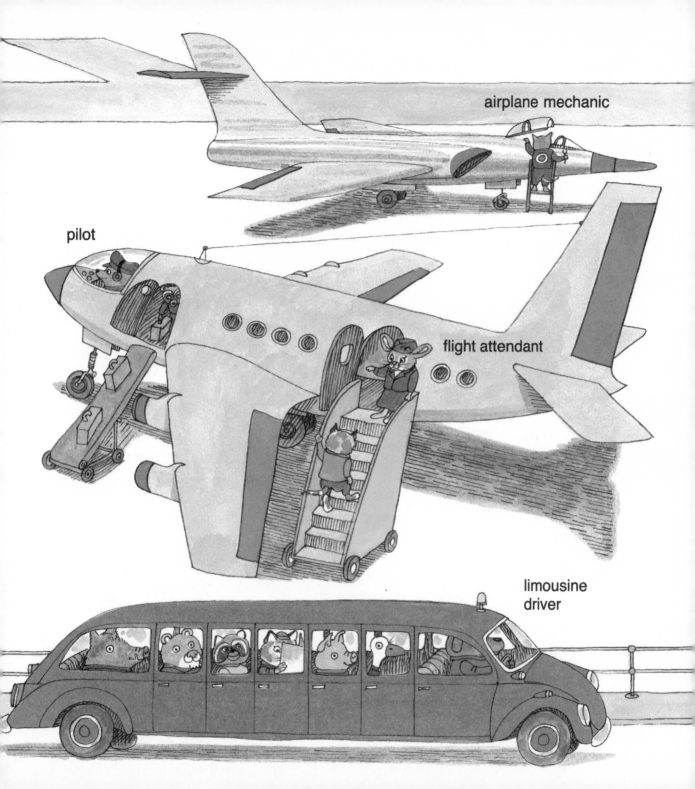

airplane mechanic

pilot

flight attendant

limousine driver

tanker truck driver

When a car stops at the gas station, workers fill the gas tank and check the oil. Gas is brought to the station in a big tanker and stored underground. Then the attendant pumps gas from the underground tank to the car.

car wash attendant

CAR WASH

gas attendant

Here comes the tow truck with a broken-down car. The mechanics will use their tools to repair it.

tow truck driver

auto mechanic

excavator operator

crane operator

backhoe operator

flatbed truck driver

It's a busy day at the construction site. First the workers will dig a ditch. Then the crane will lower a water pipe into the ground. When the work is done, water will flow through the pipe to people's homes.

bulldozer operator

lumberjack

The lumberjack is chopping down
a big tree with his ax.

forklift
driver

Once the tree is cut down, the forklift
driver gathers the big logs.

log-loader
operator

A log-loading crane picks
up the logs and puts them
on a truck. The truck will
take the logs to the sawmil
where they will be cut
into wooden boards.

Wood is used to build many things.
The carpenter uses wood to build a house.

carpenter

toy maker

The toy maker uses wood
to make a toy wagon.

The boatbuilder is building
a wooden rowboat.

boatbuilder

furniture maker

Oh, dear. The furniture maker
made a chair. But something
is wrong with it.
Do you see what it is?

butcher

MEATS

manager

cashier

NUTS

stock clerk

assistant manager

clerk

VEGETABLES

The workers at the supermarket make shopping
pleasant and easy. The assistant manager weighs
fruits and vegetables. Other workers make sure
the shelves are full of food.

Oops! Someone spilled some milk on the floor.
One of the clerks quickly mops it up.

waitress

It's such a treat to eat in a restaurant. The waiters, waitresses, and cooks work very hard to make the meal enjoyable.

waiter

hungry diners

busboy

cook

baker

The baker has had a busy day.
Look at all the pies he has baked.

dishwasher

Schtoompah is taking his big tuba
out of the closet. He is going
to play it in the band concert.

Look at all the musicians.
They make everyone happy
by playing wonderful music.

drummer

guitarist

tuba player

conductor

saxophonist

trumpeter

Glip and Glop are painters.
They have come to paint
Mrs. Pig's house.

painter

Glop is painting
a funny-looking wolf
on Percy's bedroom wall.

They paint a big happy sun on
the bedroom ceiling.
What a wonderful way
to brighten up the room.

dentist

Some workers help you stay healthy.
The dentist cleans and takes care
of your teeth.

When you're not feeling well,
the doctor examines you to find
out what is wrong.

doct

nurse

At the hospital
the nurse gives
a sick patient
his medicine.

teacher

artist

student

principal

In the classroom you'll find lots of busy students.
They are learning to read, write, and paint.
The principal is happy to see the students
working so hard.

The world is full of busy workers. Look around your town. What busy workers do you see?

There are many different kinds of jobs. What kind of busy worker would you like to be when you grow up?